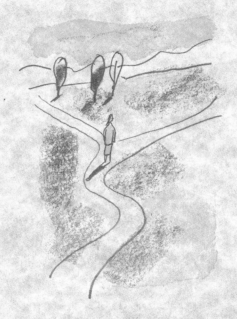

I dwell in possibilities.

———————

Emily Dickinson (1830–1886)
American poet

19   18   17   16   15   14   13   12   11   10
Digit on the right indicates the number of this printing.

ISBN 1–56138–699–5

Illustrations by Diane Bigda
Designed by Susan E. Van Horn
Edited by Tara Ann McFadden, with research by Joan McIntosh
Printed in the United States

This book may be ordered by mail from the publisher.
Please add $2.50 for postage and handling.
But try your bookstore first!

Running Press Book Publishers
125 South Twenty-second Street
Philadelphia, Pennsylvania 19103–4399

PASSAGES

JOURNAL

A personal notebook with quotes on growth, change, and understanding

RUNNING PRESS
PHILADELPHIA · LONDON

Life is not complex. We are complex.
Life is simple, and the simple thing is the right thing.

———————

Oscar Wilde (1854–1900)
Irish poet and playwright

You gain strength, courage, and confidence by every
experience in which you really stop to look fear in the face.

————

Eleanor Roosevelt (1884–1962)
American stateswoman and humanitarian

If you have made mistakes . . . there is always
another chance for you. . . . You may have a fresh start any
moment you choose, for this thing we call "failure" is not
the falling down, but the staying down.

Mary Pickford (1893–1979)
American actress

The world is a rose; smell it and pass it to your friends.

————————

Persian proverb

Only in growth, reform, and change, paradoxically enough, is true security to be found.

——————

Anne Morrow Lindbergh (b. 1906)
American writer, poet, and aviator

In the midst of winter, I finally learned
that there was in me an invincible summer.

———————

Albert Camus (1913–1960)
French writer

We are all pilgrims on the same journey . . .
but some pilgrims have better road maps.

—————

Nelson De Mille (b. 1943)
American writer

It doesn't matter if the water is cold or warm
if you're going to have to wade through it anyway.

———————

Teilhard de Chardin (1881–1955)
French paleontologist and philosopher

That is what learning is. You suddenly
understand something you've understood
all your life, but in a new way.

———

Doris Lessing (b. 1919)
English writer

Real development is not leaving things behind,
as on a road, but drawing life from them, as from a root.

———————

G. K. Chesterton (1874–1936)
English writer

People think you have to be going some place,
when, in fact, the ride is plenty.

———————

Ann Patchett (b. 1963)
American writer

I learn by going where I have to go.

Theodore Roethke (1908–1963)
American poet

The events of childhood do not pass,
but repeat themselves like seasons of the year.

———

Eleanor Farjeon (1881–1965)
English writer

You were once wild here. Don't let them tame you!

Isadora Duncan (1878–1927)
American dancer

Each day, and the living of it, has to be a conscious creation in which discipline and order are relieved with some play and pure foolishness.

———

May Sarton (1912–1995)
Belgian-born American writer

The years teach much which the days never know.

Ralph Waldo Emerson (1803–1882)
American writer

A thought may touch the edge of our life with light.

———————

John Trowbridge (1827–1916)
American writer

A̶ccept the pain, cherish the joys, resolve the regrets;
then can come the best of benedictions—"If I had my life
to live over, I'd do it all the same."

———

Joan McIntosh (b. 1943)
American writer

All glory comes from daring to begin.

—————

Anonymous

If you don't experience your life, you're not going
to come up with solutions for anything.
Every intention, every achievement has come
out of dissatisfaction, not serenity. No one ever said,
"Things are perfect. Let's invent fire."

Fran Lebowitz (b. 1951)
American writer

Life seems to be a never-ending
series of survivals, doesn't it?

———————

Carroll Baker (b. 1931)
American actress and writer

Experience is not what happens to you;
it is what you do with what happens to you.

———

Aldous Huxley (1894–1963)
English writer

W hen we can begin to take our failures
non-seriously, it means we are ceasing to be afraid
of them. It is of immense importance to learn
to laugh at ourselves.

————

Katherine Mansfield (1888–1923)
New Zealand-born English writer

If I were to begin life again, I should want it as it were.
I would only open my eyes a little more.

———————

Jules Renard (1864–1910)
French writer

From without, no wonderful effect is wrought
within ourselves unless some interior, responding
wonder meets it.

———————

Herman Melville (1819–1891)
American writer

Growth, in some curious way, I suspect,
depends on being always in motion just a little bit,
one way or another.

————

Norman Mailer (b. 1923)
American writer

Some trees grow very tall and straight and large
in the forest close to each other, but some must stand
by themselves or they won't grow at all.

———

Oliver Wendell Holmes (1809–1894)
American writer

When the most important things in our life happen, we quite often do not know, at the moment, what is going on.

————

C. S. Lewis (1898–1963)
English writer

W**hat would life be if we had no courage
to attempt anything?**

———

*Vincent Van Gogh (1853–1890)
Dutch painter*

If we are always arriving and departing,
it is also true that we are eternally anchored.
One's destination is never a place, but rather
a new way of looking at things.

———————

Henry Miller (1891–1980)
American writer

The events in our lives happen in a sequence
in time, but in their significance to ourselves, they
find their own order . . . the continuous thread
of revelation.

Eudora Welty (b. 1909)
American writer

Do not think your truth can be found by anyone else.

André Gide (1869–1951)
French writer

Everyone has a talent. What is rare is the courage
to follow the talent to the dark place where it leads.

———

Erica Jong (b. 1942)
American writer

I began to have an idea of my life, not as the slow shaping of achievement to fit my preconceived purposes, but as the gradual discovery and growth of a purpose which I did not know.

———

Joanna Field (b. 1900)
English psychologist

Very little is needed to make a happy life.
It is all within yourself, in your way of thinking.

———————

Marcus Aurelius (121–180)
Roman emperor and philosopher

Be not afraid of growing slowly;
be afraid only of standing still.

———

Chinese proverb

Nothing is so often irretrievably missed
as a daily opportunity.

Marie von Ebner-Eschenbach (1830–1916)
Austrian writer

Perspective, I soon realized, was a fine
commodity, but utterly useless when I was
in the thick of things.

———————

Ingrid Bengis (b. 1944)
American writer

If only I may grow: firmer, simpler—quieter, warmer.

———————

Dag Hammarskjöld (1905–1961)
Swedish statesman and humanitarian

It is not how much we have, but how much we enjoy, that makes happiness.

——————

Charles H. Spurgeon (1834–1892)
English cleric

No one remains quite what he was when
he recognizes himself.

———

Thomas Mann (1875–1955)
German writer

Far away there in the sunshine are my
highest aspirations. I may not reach them,
but I can look up and see their beauty,
believe in them, and try to follow
where they lead.

————

Louisa May Alcott (1832–1888)
American writer

I was raised to sense what someone wanted me to be and be that kind of person. It took me a long time not to judge myself through someone else's eyes.

———————

Sally Field (b. 1946)
American actress

You have to choose the voice you are going to trust.
You can't listen to everyone.

———————

Alice Hoffman (b. 1952)
American writer

A life spent in making mistakes is not
only more honorable but more useful than
a life spent in doing nothing.

———————

George Bernard Shaw (1856–1950)
Irish dramatist and critic

W̶e move ahead by going deeper.

———

Jennifer James (b. 1943)
American writer

There are two rules in life. . . .
One, things never work out all the way.
And two, they always turn around.

———

James Webb (1946–1980)
Scottish writer

I am incapable of conceiving infinity, and yet I do not accept finity. I want this adventure that is the context of my life to go on without end.

─────────

Simone de Beauvoir (1908–1986)
French writer

It's not when you realize that nothing can help you—
religion, pride, anything—it's when you realize you
don't need any aid.

———————

William Faulkner (1897–1962)
American writer

I think it's the end of progress if you stand still
and think of what you've done in the past. I keep on.

———

Leslie Caron (b. 1931)
French actress

If we choose to remain ourselves, full of potential,
then we can take whatever happens and redeem it by
openness, courage, and willingness to move on. . . .

———————

Madeleine L'Engle (b. 1918)
American writer

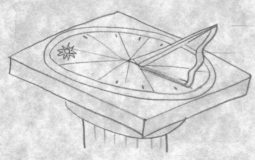

Life can only be understood backwards,
but it must be lived forwards.

Søren Kierkegaard (1813–1855)
Danish philosopher

E verything in life that we really accept
undergoes a change.

———————

Katherine Mansfield (1888–1923)
English writer

One thing I had to learn was that
nothing remains the same . . . people
grow and change. . . . You look
around and somebody is different
from a year earlier.

————

Barbara Mandrell (b. 1948)
American singer

If we could be twice young and twice old,
we could correct all our mistakes.

———————

Euripides (c. 484–406 B.C.)
Greek dramatist

If fate throws a knife at you, there are two
ways of catching it—by the blade and by the handle.

————————

Oriental proverb

The day will happen whether or not you get up.

John Ciardi (1916–1985)
American poet and critic

That which we are, we are, and if we are ever to be
any better, now is the time to begin.

———

Alfred, Lord Tennyson (1809–1892)
English poet

Mingle a little folly with your wisdom; a little
nonsense now and then is pleasant.

———

Horace (65–8 B.C.)
Roman poet and satirist

Reality was much prettier than a dream.

————

Carolina Maria de Jesus
20th-century Brazilian poet and writer

Habit is habit, and not to be flung out the window by man, but coaxed downstairs a step at a time.

———————

Mark Twain (1835–1910)
American writer

It isn't so much that hard times are coming; the change observed is mostly soft times going.

———

Groucho Marx (1890–1977)
American humorist, actor, and writer

Trying to define yourself is like trying
to bite your own teeth.

————

Alan Watts (b. 1915)
American philosopher

You do not notice changes in what is before you.

———————

Colette [Sidonie-Gabrielle] (1873–1954)
French writer

The best we can do for one another is to exchange our thoughts freely; and that, after all, is about all.

———

James A. Froude (1818–1894)
English historian

The important thing is not to stop questioning.

Albert Einstein (1879–1955)
German-born American physicist

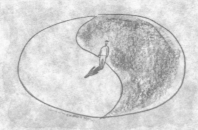

We are made out of oppositions; we live between
two poles . . . you don't reconcile the poles,
you just recognize them.

———————

Orson Welles (1915–1985)
American film director

To know ourselves is to know who we were, but who
we are or who we might become is never certain.

———

Deena Metzger (b. 1936)
American writer

. . . words are a form of action, capable of influencing
change. Their articulation represents a complete,
lived experience.

———

Ingrid Bengis (b. 1944)
American writer

To know how to grow old is the master work of wisdom, and one of the most difficult chapters in the great art of living.

———

Henri Frédéric Amiel (1821–1881)
Swiss poet and philosopher

Our greatest glory consists, not in never falling,
but in rising every time we fall.

_____

Oliver Goldsmith (1728–1774)
English poet and writer

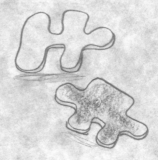

For every problem there is one solution
which is simple, neat, and wrong.

———

H. L. Mencken (1880–1956)
American editor and satirist

The best way out is always through.

———

Robert Frost (1874–1963)
American poet

You decide to do something, perform one small action, and suddenly it's a tide, the momentum is going, and there's no possibility of turning back. Somehow, even though you thought you foresaw all that would happen, you didn't know the pace would pick up so.

Amanda Cross (b. 1926)
American writer

Y̶ou can't change the music of your soul.

———

Katharine Hepburn (b. 1909)
American actress

I've dreamt in my life dreams that have stayed
with me ever after, and changed my ideas; they've
gone through and through me, like wine through
water, and altered the colour of my mind.

Emily Brontë (1818–1848)
English writer

Of all the liars in the world, sometimes the worst
are your own fears.

———

Rudyard Kipling (1865–1936)
English poet and writer

When you're an orthodox worrier,
some days are worse than others.

———

Erma Bombeck (1927–1996)
American writer

And what made it worse was the blurry knowledge that, once she had chosen, she would forget there had ever been a choice. From the crossroads at the crest of the hill you can see in every direction; but after you start down one of the paths the view narrows, and other landscapes vanish.

———————

Alison Lurie (b. 1926)
American writer

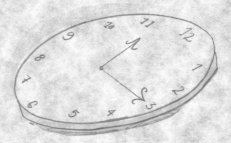

Nothing is as far away as one minute ago.

————————

Jim Bishop (1907–1987)
American writer

To feel that one has a place in life solves
half the problem of contentment.

———————

George E. Woodberry (1855–1930)
American writer

Anything you're good at contributes to happiness.

———

Bertrand Russell (1872–1970)
English mathematician and philosopher

. . . a talent is something given, that opens like
a flower, but without exceptional energy, discipline,
and persistence will never bear fruit.

———

May Sarton (1912–1995)
Belgian-born American writer

We grow in time to trust the future for our answers.

—————

Ruth Benedict (1887–1948)
American anthropologist

The difficulty in life is the choice.

George Moore (1852–1933)
Irish writer

What you get is a living—what you give is a life.

———

Lillian Gish (1896–1993)
American actress

. . . an "in-between" zone, a state in which we are
neither who we used to be, nor who we are becoming.
It's like standing in a doorway, or being in a
passageway, or even in a long dark tunnel, between
two phases of our lives.

————

Jean Shinoda Bolen
20th-century American educator and writer

People change and forget to tell each other.

Lillian Hellman (1907–1984)
American writer and playwright

We are adventuring in the chartless seas of imagination.

———

Anne Morrow Lindbergh (b. 1906)
American writer, poet, aviator

Any life, no matter how long and complex it may be, is made up of a single moment—the moment is which a man finds out, once and for all, who he is.

. . . be glad you had the moment.

Steve Shagan (b. 1927)
American screenwriter and film producer